Take the
**unexpected
path**

FIESTA
of HAPPINESS

Take the
unexpected
path

David Baird

Andrews McMeel
Publishing
Kansas City

Introduction

Nothing can lay us humans as wide open as the sudden arrival of
An unexpected event.
What better way to get the sense of someone's
Character than by observing them in a state of surprise?
Especially those great organizers among us . . .
You know, the ones who are never in a hurry,
Never late for an appointment,
Never forget an anniversary.
They are the cautious ones,
Who avoid even dipping their toe in water
And to whom the unexpected is not only unsettling, but

Unprepared for.
Are these people happy?
I don't think so.
But what of those people we meet, who,
Beaming with happiness,
Hold us mesmerized from the moment
They utter the little phrase:
"You'll never guess what happened to me today!"
The ones who regularly travel the
Unexpected path.
Why not follow them?

Paint a mental picture

Get out of town for the day
Out to where the air is clean,
The paths are quiet
And where all signs of man's interference with nature are
Out of sight.
Look, really look, about when you're there
And pick a spot to be your very own spot.
Bury something you love at that place . . .
A coin, a bead . . . something simple,
Then look again until you can close your eyes
And remember it just as it is.
From that point on in life you'll know
You have a little picture in your mind
Of a quiet place
Where you can go at will
Just by closing your eyes.

Turn on and tune in

Make today a voyage of discovery.
Peer over those railings and
Peek down that stairwell.
See what the rest of the world has going on.
Turn on and tune in,
Listen to what's going on around you.
There's a different pulse to each moment and
Brand-new life in every day.
There's a symphony in each and every one of us
Just waiting to be performed.

Who dares wins

Sometimes we can win in life
And sometimes we feel we lose.
But the chance is the thing,
That exhilarating thrill that comes
Whether we win or lose.
And provided we don't go out
Recklessly investing all our worldly possessions in
No-hope schemes,
We can still enjoy the thrills and spills of taking chances
And find pleasure in others' good fortune.

A little existentialism

Let the world know that you exist.
Even in the line at the bakery
Your presence can change
The flow of the day.
Avoid routine and create some new ones . . .
Give up your train seat during rush hour,
Stand still,
Look up at the architecture that you hurry by each day,
And watch the chain reaction.
You exist . . .
Yes you do!

Seize every moment

Gone . . .
That moment came and went
Before we could even think about it
And so will the next one.
You see?
Moments are like waves in the ocean of life:
Some people ignore them,
Some watch them,
Others surf them.
Grab your surfboard and
Ride the next moment!

Designs on life

Be the architect of your moment.
Plant a garden in your imagination,
Let the trees and flowers
Tower above the rooftops,
Then rearrange the houses
In your neighborhood,
Choose a vibrant new door color,
Change the ring of your doorbell,
Become the architect of your moment.

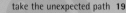

Downtown Drama

Have a
High Street Adventure.
Spread some smiles
Among the passersby.
And if the conditions are right
You might even risk a few
Hellos along the way.

Color the day

Splash out
And bring a flash of color into your day.
If everything seems dull around you
And too gray to bear,
Why not change it?
Dress your day in colors
That contrast with what you see.
If there's a line of bare winter trees
Standing in a gloomy row,
Tie a ribbon to one of them
And see how the whole picture changes.

Join the audience

Sometimes
When everything seems too much
It helps to become
A member of the audience
For the show of life.
Hunt out a snug little bistro
Or café in a bustling street
And simply sit there
Watching the world go by.

Save a life...

Look kindly on that poor little moth
That's been stuck in your bathroom for two days
Let it out into the big wide world
And feel yourself a freedom fighter.

Get out there

Each day we have the choice to:
Stay in or go out.
Stay in too often and you can fall into the habit of
Staying in every day.
Zip off somewhere instead . . .
Go to the station and buy a day ticket
To somewhere unknown . . .
And a whole world of new discoveries
Awaits you.
Shop in a different store,
Eat at a different café . . .
Wearing different shoes
And walk out into a new, undiscovered day . . .
The memory of which will last you
A lifetime.

Beauty

Try and find beauty in everything today
And beauty will find you.
We can all be surprised
When we take down
Our barriers of preconception
By what the world and those in it have to offer.
A beautiful day,
A beautiful idea,
A beautiful thought,
A beautiful deed.

Connect with the crowd

Collect smiles,
Or hellos from passersby
As you walk the length of a crowded street.
Look into any sea of faces and you can be guaranteed
To discover hundreds who, like you,
Are yearning to communicate with others and
Share in a moment of human interaction.
After the first two or three experiments
It soon becomes easy to spot who's up for this,
And, you know what?
It's infectious.

Artistic License

Be creative, starting with
How you style your hair in the morning,
The way you set the breakfast table,
Adding a few roses or some melon balls!
Drape a scarf round your neck à la Parisian
As you head out into the world
Release the artist in you and
Let your eyes become the paintbrushes of your day.
Broad strokes for the sky,
Fine detail for the ironwork.

At the office—
Get creative with the photocopier
Collaborate with your computer,
Get a few gifs in your life
And don't let jpegs be your hang-up!
A whole new perception of you
Can be simply created
With a new way of greeting people
On the telephone.

Today is "no rush" day

Unplug the phone—
Take up a meditation pose and sit.
Then, relax and let everything go . . . go . . . go
Until your body becomes like just so many bubbles.
Feel yourself fall into timelessness.
When you enter deepest meditation
Your Inner Being will become wrapped
In Being, Itself.
Feel the material world vanish.
While sitting in meditation
Make the journey to the place of no doubts.
Experience being detached from all that can be possessed
And in your state of "poverty"
You will have a few moments to attain
All that is valuable under heaven.

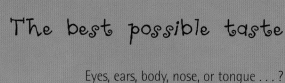

The best possible taste

Eyes, ears, body, nose, or tongue . . . ?
It's devilishly difficult to say
Which of these is the most amazing.
What if we were to dedicate a day to each?
Perhaps start with the tongue
And try all manner of different things that it can
Savor . . . a new blend of coffee
Something as yet untried or new on the menu.
When was the last time (if ever) that you
Stood still in the rain
And allowed your tongue to catch a raindrop?
How did it feel and how does it taste?
At the end of your day's journey of taste bud travel,
Why not use it one last time
To lick a stamp and send an unexpected card
To a long-forgotten friend.

Change the old routine!

We live in a beautiful world.
Aim to see as much of it as you can.
The well-worn route we take every day
Is not necessarily the best,
Or the fastest,
Or even going in the right direction!
We're just used to it.
Change down a gear and cruise the roads
You generally would speed down.
Take the scenic route for once.
If you want to get to somewhere new in your life,
You have to risk taking an
Unfamiliar turn.

Be a daredevil

How do you treat yourself?
With kid gloves?
Have you ever calculated
That for about the same cost as a weekend away
In a single-star hotel
Or a slap-up feast
At your local restaurant,
You could have an adventure
That will sparkle in your memory
For the remainder of your days?
Think of it.
Piloting a Tiger Moth,
Diving with dolphins, or driving a racing car.
Make time to do one thing—several things—
In your lifetime
That you never dreamed you'd do.

Are you in the pink?

At any time of the year
  It's wonderful to look out
  At the colors of the world.
  Each new season seems secure
  In its own colors, and the way we feel at
Different times of the year suggests we have
Some form of seasonal response.
  Could it be, do you suppose, that our reactions are
  Color-coded?
  If so, don't feel blue.
    Perk yourself up with a strawberry attitude
    And place yourself under saffron sun.
      As though it were the height of summer—
        Life will surely look rosier.

Take a saintly path

There is one exquisite truth in life
Which is that all saints and ordinary folk
Start out the same in life.
So why not be a saint for a day?
Choose your moment and set off along the saintly path.
Explore your feelings, beliefs, and truths as you travel
To discover what saintliness means for you
And how differently you treat your fellow travelers.
If you find you're happier than ever before,
You can decide to make this your path for life.

The height of delight

Make a moment in your schedule to whisk yourself away
To a place where, without any need for
Crampons and ropes, you are way above sea level.
Get nearer the clouds . . . up in the sky.
The top of a windswept hill
Or, better still, a towering mountain.
As you climb, feel your heart pull away from
All its worldly attachments, and when you are
On the peak amid the clouds,
Let your body stand strong and true on its own.

Lights! Camera! Action!

It's the first day on set today.
The film is a black-and-white classic with you as the star.
See how long you can pull off playing the part
Of your favorite film role.
Saying the sorts of things that character would have said
Wearing the styles that actor might have worn.
Order coffee as Marlene Dietrich
Or Cary Grant
Do the length of Main Street
As Mary Poppins or James Bond.
How would Spencer Tracy deal
With the man on the telephone
From the gas company?

Clear out inner clutter

In a state of complete calm and utter honesty
Face yourself and your life
And go through both piece by piece.
Seek out all the little embellishments and untruths
That have accumulated over the years,
And have a good clearout.
You need to create room in your heart . . .
A big empty space where you can store away
The handful of things that matter most to you,
That are pure and good and faithful and true.

The point of it

We live in a constant state of communication these days.

Who hasn't got a mobile phone or e-mail?

When was the last time you went a whole day without

E-mailing or being e-mailed?

All too many of us rush to contact someone else

To describe something we're living or experiencing.

Well switch off that phone!

Think about it,

As you're struggling to describe it,

You're missing the whole point.

The thing is to live it . . .

To get the point of it . . .

Unlike the chap who,

Standing in front of a display of newly arrived exotic fruits

Completely unknown to him,

Reaches for his mobile phone.

Come out into the light

Who says that every day
Has to be the same?
Each morning
Sees us born into a new day.
Not only us.
Each dawn
The sun rises naked and new
As a babe.
If you want to share
In the incredible lightness of being
Go out into the day,
Open yourself up
And let that sunlight
Stream into your life.

Brave new worlds

What is there
That other people do
That you have never even considered doing?
If you truly want to distance yourself
From the familiar
Take yourself off on a discovery day
Try a day at the racetrack
Or a night out at the opera.
Pack some lunch
And spend the day watching a baseball game,
Sit in on a lecture,
Or go to a boot sale.
Open yourself to the experience
And be aware of those around you.
Especially yourself.

Lazing about on the river

Steer your attention to that famous children's story
The Wind in the Willows,
And take a leaf out of the good old water rat's book.
Arm yourself with a bursting picnic basket,
Plus a good friend and head off to the river
And make a long day of it.
Take along a wind-up gramophone, or, better still,
A ukulele, and feel pressures accumulated over
Days, weeks, even years
Dissolve
As you drift along.
There's nothing, absolutely nothing,
Half so worth doing.
Nice? It's the *only* thing.

Ins and outs

We all consist of a within
And we all consist of a without.
So far so good.
Two aspects of ourselves that are so closely related
Yet also independent.
Both work in different ways
Yet affect each other deeply.
Our physical body must interact with our thoughts,
But we experience our thoughts as being
Independent of the physical world.
It's a two-way street
Going in the same direction.
If you don't believe it,
Try doing anything without thinking.

The sweet smell of success

Just as the bud must give up its youth
In order to flower
So it can release its fragrance
Into the world, so we, too
Must let go of the past
If we are to bloom
And release the perfume of our flowers.

Don't ossify—diversify!

Remember there are no strict rules.
At no time does someone come up to you and say:
"That's it! That's who you are . . .
That's what your life is,"
And expect you to reflect that fact
Until the end of your days.
Why shouldn't a traffic cop
Be a tabla player on weekends
Or a nursery-school teacher
Be a free-fall parachutist?
All it takes is your own imagination
Seasoned with a sprinkling of
Go For It!

Give peace a chance

All of us want to find
Peace in our lives.
The strange thing is that the more we strive
To attain it, the more elusive it seems.
Instead you have to let go.
If you let go a little, you'll have a little peace.
If you let go a lot, you'll have a lot of peace.
If you let go completely, you'll have complete peace.

Companion piece

Focus on a friend—
Someone who has been faithfully
Beside you over the years,
Someone you have rummaged
And combed the beaches together with.
Select the friend who has created in you
An ever-bubbling spring of precious friendship
That will flow forever,
And dedicate a day to him or her
And your special bond.

Up, up, and away

Anyone can sit around
Watching the temperature drop
As autumn sets in.
The happy few, instead of complaining about it,
Get airborne on a bright frosty morning
In a hot-air balloon.
Way up there you can see life
From a wholly different perspective.
As you rise
Then drift along silently
Gaze down on the world below
And reflect on the imprint your life has made upon it.

Monkey business

An inspiring sight
Can be seen each day
In China
As young and old,
Rich and poor alike,
Gather in the parks and en masse
Slip into the slow-motion world
Of Tai Chi.
This graceful and thoughtfully performed movement sequence
With names like
Step Back And Repulse Monkey,
Is remarkably rewarding.
It promotes focus, balance,
Memory, circulation, and general well-being.
There will be a class you can attend
Wherever you are in the world.

Make like a maverick

It's by defying logic, breaking the mold
And taking off at a tangent
That inventor and entrepreneurs come up with
A lightbulb, a CD, a Post-it note.
It's by challenging the odds, applying topspin,
Ignoring the norm, combining opposites,
That heroes are made, runs scored,
Records broken, fashions launched,
Champions born, legends created.
Take your oddball idea, your nutcase notion,
Your madcap dream,
And run with it!

Dazed and confused?

Why do we look forward longingly to holidays
Or weekends, then spend time before
Our precious break
Dashing around searching for what isn't there,
Afraid of making choices in case something
Better is just around the corner?
Stop!
Cease searching, cease choosing, and listen . . .

Indecision gives rise to confusion
And in confusion where can a mind go?
Cease searching and it will find you
Make one big decision—
To make no more unnecessary decisions.
And enjoy an unconfused and
Well-earned rest.

The usual, Sir? Madam?

Who wants to go through life being greeted with the
Query: "The Usual?"
Such predictability is hardly happiness inspiring.
Sip a few new cocktails.
Dip into unexplored regions of the menu.
Slip into different bars and
Different restaurants.
Break with routine
And become
Unusual!

Give life a lift

What you've always considered a flaw or a blot
Others may see as a beauty spot.
Why change your quirky nose to fit a stereotypical mold?
If you've got it, flaunt it!
Madonna has kept her gappy front teeth.
But if something is making you feel really low and
Afraid to face the world,
Having it treated is a sensible step.
Just look before you leap
Into liposuction, rhinoplasty, wrinkle reduction,
Whatever . . .
Be sure you trust the expert, and remember the
Hitchhiker's guide:
"Never accept a lift from a stranger!"

A la carte

How many menus do you have in you?
What exactly is the full extent of your gastronomic repertoire,
Your culinary capabilities?
Most of the television cookery programs that have
Taken the viewing world by storm are prepared for and
Served up to a faithful audience of
Kitchen wanna-bes perched on the edge of their sofas
Trying to take in the recipe for beef Wellington while
Balancing a plate of beans on toast on their laps!
Why not enroll in a cookery course?
Show you're an egghead and excel at rocket science.
Wow the world with your salad power dressing.
Set friends swooning over your sushi, then
Bedazzle them with your banana splits!

Say yes for success

If you always say no,
The invitations cease to flow.
Ruts grow deeper
Hurdles higher.
Fears are overcome by doing the very things
You fear.
If you always do what you've always done,
You'll always have what you always had.
But walk the tightrope,
Unlock that door,
And things can only get better.

Change up a gear

If you're stuck in one of life's pit stops,

You may not need a whole new engine—

Just a little fine-tuning here and there.

The simplest changes can spark our brain cells

Into functioning like a Ferrari.

So wear your watch on the other wrist,

Take a different route to work,

Carry your bag in the other hand,

Buy an untried newspaper . . .

Notice how weird you feel at first

But welcome the new willingness it brings

To try out alternative things

And watch your life zoom off with a va-va-voom!

How to think

Happiness cannot be found by thinking
Other people's thoughts.
A good teacher will not teach us what to think, but
How to think!
A person's life is what their thoughts make of it.
You are today
Where your thoughts have brought you;
And you will be tomorrow
Where your thoughts transport you.
Thoughts have no substance in themselves—
Ignore them and they'll go away—but,
Give a thought your undivided attention
And it can fill
An ocean.

A sound investment

If you want to get through life
Avoiding all the false dogmas and doctrines
That can deafen us,
If you want a guaranteed return
From an investment,
What better decision could there be than to invest in
Yourself?
An investment in such a proposition
Will give you a sense of security
Through boom and bust, bubble and trouble.
Trust in yourself and reap the profits
Throughout your life.

The facts of life

Sometimes we get mightily confused between
What constitutes a problem
And what is a fact.
Try looking at it this way:
If your problem has no solution
Stop your fretting and consider that
It might not be a problem at all,
But may, in fact, be a fact!
Facts aren't meant to be solved.
They're something we cope with,
Like going through life with big feet.
A problem, on the other hand,
Is more like a leaky bathtub
And requires the intervention of a plumber!

Change

The prayer of mankind goes something like this:
"Let me see something tomorrow that
I have never seen before!"
It's curious that people seem to be
Most happy when they're looking forward to
Something new, something different,
But almost as soon as the new arrives
It becomes old and stale and *so* last season.
And the next wish forms—

Which is for
Something new, something different.
It's like travel or coffee:
Both seem best in the anticipation
Or the remembering,
Not the actual experience.
Let your Next Big Thing be to buck the trend
And treasure today's Big Thing.

Find the connection

How often do we go out of our way to get to know
People as people . . . as individuals?
Especially the ones who seem different from us.
We find working with them, living near them,
How they look and how they make us feel,
Disturbing.
It's easy to put up our defenses.
But if we bring them down and try to find
Common ground,
Unexpected connections and unforeseen friendships can form.
Remember that some have welcomed strangers
Into their homes and entertained
Angels unawares.

Discovery channel

Here's to those

Who try to master circumstances

And attempt to do everything

Better than it's ever been done before.

And to those who live to do the right thing,

The right way, at the right time.

Our only wish for you is

That within your busy schedule

You create some opportunities for yourselves,

Room for happiness, time

To take some uninhibited risks,

Space to make mistakes that

Often lead to sensational places.

Novelty factor

It's the hectic, complicated, overcrowded life
That is the most memorable.
A life that's been full of wrong turns,
Failures alongside achievements,
Disappointments alongside joys,
The occasional crisis, some pleasant surprises,
And some unpleasant ones.
These are the riveting chapters of a full life story.
Edit them out
And you'd have a putdownable dull tale.
So jump off the shelf and make your life
A real page turner!

What did you expect?

The joke of mankind is that
History keeps on repeating itself
Yet mankind never seems to learn from experience
Not to be caught out by the unexpected.
The twist is that if you go out
Expecting the unexpected,
You will not meet it,
Because it wants to catch you off-guard.
The trick is to become an expert in the unexpected
Through practicing.
Keep on varying your routine,
Doing what comes *un*naturally,
And you'll soon excel at being
Unfazed by the unexpected.

Trivial pursuits

Is what you are about to do important?
How will you look back on it in years to come?
We rarely seem to think about it but
At some point in everybody's allotted life span they will do
The most important work of their life.
For you it might be today!
Think about this and perhaps from now on
You'll be less inclined
To just trundle along through life
Spending vast chunks of time
Doing trivial things.

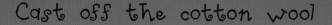

Cast off the cotton wool

Have you ever watched someone go through life
Afraid to do anything new or try out anything daring
In case they get hurt?
They're usually the first people to stub their toe
Or slip on that banana skin.
Whereas those who get out there and at it have
No such worries and seem to escape with just
A few scratches.
Why?
Because they have learned that
What we fear is frequently less painful
Than we imagined,
And often a bruised eye—or pride—is a price
Worth paying.

A spoonful of sugar

That which we forecast seldom occurs.

It's a bitter pill to swallow . . .

But here comes the spoonful of sugar.

Most, if not all, of our pleasures

Are virtually guaranteed to come

From unexpected sources.

Centuries of discoveries have shown that what is

Least expected to occur is what generally happens,

And chance and coincidence play major roles.

So relax.

And accept what the Sugarplum Fairy brings you.

And in the end

Wake up . . .
Take a look in the newspaper
And if you can't see your name
In the Obituaries column,
The chances are that you're still alive
And still a vital part of this wonderful
Infinite process of being.
Don't be one of those who miss too many
Todays through worrying about the tomorrows
And are always planning
To start living tomorrow.
Live life to the fullest today!
And when the end comes, have
Great expectations of whatever may lie
Beyond . . .

First published by **MQ Publications Limited**
12 The Ivories, 6-8 Northampton St., London, N1 2HY

Copyright © 2003 MQ Publications Limited
Text © 2003 **David Baird**
Design: **Balley Design Associates**

ISBN: 0-7407-3543-8

Library of Congress Control Number on file